SAINT IGNATIUS LOYOLA

A THOUGHT

FOR EACH DAY OF THE YEAR

Translated from the French by
Margaret A. Colton
1887

Edited by Darrell Wright, 2016

JANUARY

Jan. 1
ALL FOR THE GREATER GLORY OF GOD.
St. Ignatius repeats these words three hundred and seventy-six times in his Constitutions.

Jan. 2
Spiritual Exercises are all that I can conceive, feel, and understand to be the best in this life, either for the personal advancement of each one, or for the benefit, aid, and spiritual advantages that may be drawn from them for others. - *Letter* 10.

Jan. 3
If the devil tempts me by the thought of Divine justice, I think of God's mercy; if he tries to fill me with presumption by the thought of His mercy, I think of His justice. - *Letter* 8.

Jan. 4

One of the most admirable effects of Holy Communion is to preserve souls from sin, and to help those who fall through weakness to rise again; it is much more profitable, then, to approach this Divine Sacrament often with love, respect, and confidence, than to remain away through an excess of fear and scrupulousness. - *Letter* 21.

Jan. 5

Provided that humility and sweet-ness are not lacking in you, the good - ness of God will not fail to help you to fulfill, not only without repugnance, but even with joy, whatever promises you have made Him. - *Letter on Obedience.*

Jan. 6

What I wish above all is, that you

busy yourselves in the pure love of
Jesus Christ, in the desire for His
glory, and the salvation of souls which
He has so dearly purchased. - *Letter* 50.

Jan. 7
One who is ill must not wish to do
the work of a well man; let him
compensate by moderation and patience, and not injure his health.
- Nolarci, *Life of St Ignatius of Loyola.*

Jan. 8
I love to see the good in health,
the wicked ill; the former because
they consecrate their strength to
the glory of God, the latter for the
excess of evil they return to Him.
- Ribadeneira, *Life of Ignatius of Loyola,*
Book 5, ch. 2.

Jan. 9

I ardently desire, and I ask you by the love and respect we bear to our Divine Master, that in our spiritual exercises we would remember one another. - *Letter* 14.

Jan. 10

I do not desire to see in superiors all the emotions of the soul, and above all those of anger, extinguished and entirely destroyed, but I want them perfectly subdued. - *Life*, Book 3, n. 46.

Jan. 11

One must wage war against his predominant passion and not retreat until, with God's help, he has been victorious. - Maffaei, Book 3, ch. 1.

Jan. 12

It is God's love for us whence flows

all the bitterness as well as all the sweets of this lite. - *Letter* 136.

Jan. 13
More determination is required to subdue the interior man than to mortify the body; and to break one's will than to break one's bones. - Bartoli, Book 4.

Jan. 14
To use the members of a religious order for the service of God, to the violation of the rule, is to throw down a tree to gather its fruit.
- Bartoli, Book 1.

Jan. 15
Lord! what do I desire or what can I desire but Thee?
- Ribadeneira, Book 5, ch. 1.

Jan. 16

Let the apostolic man not forget himself: he has not come to handle gold, but mud; he cannot, therefore, watch himself too carefully, that he may not contract the leprosy of which he seeks to cure others. - *Life*, Book 2.

Jan. 17

The vigor with which you resist the enemy will be the measure of the reward which will follow the combat. - Ribadeneira, ch. 37.

Jan. 18

That we may not be misled by self-love in the management of our affairs, let us not consider them as our own but as another's; partiality will thus give way to justice. - Bartoli.

Jan. 19

Whilst the enemy sees us humble,
he tries to inspire the mind with a
false humility, that is to say, an extreme and wicked humility. - *Letter* 8.

Jan. 20

He who bears God in his heart,
carries his paradise with him every-
where. - *In Compendium Vitae.*

Jan. 21

Behold how the teachings of our
Lord and Savior, the Eternal Wisdom,
are rejected, His deeds forgotten,
and the price of His precious Blood
lost, in a measure, considering how few
there are who seek their salvation.
- Letter 50.

Jan. 22

As for joy, as little as one can have

of it in this life, experience shows
that it is not the idle who possess it,
but those who are zealous in the service of God. - *Letter* 5.

Jan. 23
Man has been created to praise,
honor, and serve the Lord his God,
and in this way to save his soul; and
everything else on earth exists for
man to aid him to reach the end
which God has marked out for him
in creating him. He must, then, use
things as long only as they conduct
him. to this end, and abstain from
them whenever they turn him aside
from it. - *Spiritual Exercises.*

Jan. 24
Very few men understand what
God would do for them, if they would
but give themselves entirely to Him.

- Bartoli, Book 4.

Jan. 25
He is ungrateful beyond all expres-
sion, and in heart altogether wrong,
who, in the face of God's benefits
benefits which cost Him so much
does not offer himself, and does not see
the obligation he is under to devote
himself entirely to the honor and glory
of our Lord and Savior. - *Letter* 50.

Jan. 26
It is not the finest wood that feeds
the fire of Divine love, but the wood
of the Cross. - Bartoli, Book 1.

Jan. 27
All the honey that can be gathered
from the flowers of this world has
less sweetness than the vinegar and

gall of Jesus Christ our Lord. - Bartoli.

Jan. 28
Happy are they who in this life prepare themselves to be judged and saved by Christ our Lord, who must judge us for eternity. - *Letter* 14.

Jan. 29
Love consists in an interchange of favors. To obtain the love of God, I will call to mind the favors I have received from Him. - *Spiritual Exercises.*

Jan. 30
He employs his time badly who recites long prayers, when he should use it to conquer his passions. - *Life*, Book 3, ch. 12.

Jan. 31
One great difficulty of indiscreet

fervor is to load our ship too much. It should not be empty, lest it be capsized by the storm of temptation; but to load it so that it runs aground is still worse. - *Letter* 50.

FEBRUARY

Feb. 1
If you promise to do something tomorrow, do it today.
- *Letter* 19.

Feb. 2
Regard as a temptation, and as something suspicious, all that is suggested to you contrary to God or the spirit of your institute. - Nolarci.

Feb. 3
Progress in the various spiritual ex-

ercises is in proportion to the renun-
ciation that one makes of his self-
love, his will, and all his pleasures.
- *Spiritual Exercises.*

Feb. 4

Before attacking a man, Satan
seeks the weakest or least guarded
point; then erects his battery, that
he may carry his assault.
- Bartoli, *Life of St. Ignatius of Loyola*,
Book 4, pp. 2 and 3.

Feb. 5

God is generous; I receive from
His hands what I have never received
from the hands of man; and if I
had received nothing from man, I
would receive all from God.
- Bartoli, Book 4, ch. 23.

Feb. 6

I leave it to your own judgment if
it is not best to thus make answer to
all earthly things: What do they profit
man? or to exclaim later, having
gained nothing: What do they profit
me? - *Life*, Book 2, n. 2.

Feb. 7

We ought to direct all our efforts
to reach the end which we pursue,
and once having entered on the way
of perfection, strive to gain its highest
point. - Lancidus.

Feb. 8

In the work of salvation, we must
employ against the enemy the weapons
with which he strives to destroy
us. - *History of the Society*, Book 3.

Feb. 9

Arguments and human reasoning
will never teach us as much as a
humble recourse to God. - Nolarci .

Feb. 10

There is nothing of which apostolic
men have more need than interior
recollection, in order not to endanger
their own salvation whilst seeking
that of others. - Ribadeneira, Book 3.

Feb. 11

Put a limit to your prudence, for it
is not necessary to carry to excess a
virtue which should serve to rule and
guide others. - Ribadeneira.

Feb. 12

it is not best to thus make answer to
all earthly things: What do they
profit man? or to exclaim later, hav-

ing gained nothing: "What do they profit me? - *Life*, Book 2, n. 2.

Feb. 13
We ought to direct all our efforts to reach the end which we pursue, and once having entered on the way of perfection, strive to gain its highest point. - Lancidus.

Feb. 14
In the work of salvation, we must employ against the enemy the weapons with which he strives to destroy us. - *History of the Society*, Book 3.

Feb. 15
Arguments and human reasoning will never teach us as much as a humble recourse to God. - Nolarci.

Feb. 16

There is nothing of which apostolic men have more need than interior recollection, in order not to endanger their own salvation whilst seeking that of others. - Ribadeneira, Book 3.

Feb. 17

Put a limit to your prudence, for it is not necessary to carry to excess a virtue which should serve to rule and guide others. - Ribadeneira.

Feb. 18

Our enemy is enraged when a soul discloses itself to a good confessor, or to some spiritual person who knows his cunning and wickedness, because he foresees that, his snares once discovered, he can no longer carry out his treacherous work. *Spiritual Exercises*.

Feb. 19

Take it for a principle to concede readily in the beginning of a conversation with those whose aspirations are only earthly; but reserve yourself for the end and try to cover with a layer of gold the metal of their conversation, whatsoever it may be.
- Bartoli, Book 4.

Feb. 20

A man whose heart is perverted would not know how to remain long among those who place their happiness in virtue.
- Bartoli, Book 6, ch. 37.

Feb. 21

It is not only necessary to consider what God's zeal requires in itself, but one must apply and use this zeal to the interests of his neighbor.

- Ribadeneira, ch. 47.

Feb. 22

Let the hope of one day doing great things in the service of God not make you neglect the present moment.

Feb. 23

Ask of God much suffering; in giving it to you, He will do you a great favor, for in this single gift are countless blessings.
- Bartoli, Book 4.

Feb. 24

Among all the evils and all the sins, ingratitude is, according to the best judgment, the most deserving of abhorrence on the part of God, our Lord and Creator, and of all creatures worthy of His Divine and eternal glory. - *Letter* 24.

Feb. 25
It is obligatory on us to lead to
Jesus Christ our Lord, by the most
direct and surest path, those who live
under the same roof with us. - *Letter* 34.

Feb. 26
Let us proceed joyfully and let us
be sure that all our crosses will bear
Christ with them, and that His help,
which will never be wanting to us,
will be more powerful than the com-
bined efforts of all our enemies.
- Bartoli, Book 2.

Feb. 27
I commend to you devotion in
helping your neighbor's soul in such
a manner, that you always have a

care of your own, to preserve and
perfect it in every kind of virtue to

the glory of the Lord our God.
- *Letter* 151.

Feb. 28
It is the part of Divine Goodness
to defend with greater solicitude that
which the devil attacks with most
ardor. *History of the Society*, p. 1.

MARCH

March 1.
THEY who are engaged with
the salvation of their neighbor,
will gain more by a humble
modesty than by an authoritative
manner, and will gain victory sooner

in retreat than in combat.
- *Life*, Book 4.

March 2.
Too much hatred of our neighbor's faults begets more aversion than amendment, and, far from helping him, puts him to flight.
- *Abridgment of his Life*.

March 3.
One does not speak of the works of God, even with the least of mortals, without drawing great profit from it.
- Nolarci.

March 4.
By preference, the devil attacks man at the moment of awaking; before the mind has had time for pious thoughts, he presents to it bad and forbidden ones. - Ribadeneira, ch. 37.

March 5.

Even among the present hardships
of our exile, and the wearisomeness of
our pilgrimage, obedience gives us a
foretaste of our heavenly country.
- *Letter* 51.

March 6.

It is an extreme punishment that
obliges us to remain so long on
earth, unless love causes us to live
more in Heaven and with God than
on earth and with ourselves; just as
the rays of the sun continue to shed
their light a great way off as long as
they are not separated from their
focus. - Bartoli, Book 4.

March 7.

How few there are who avail
themselves of the precious blood of
Jesus to purchase their salvation!

- Bartoli, Book 4.

March 8.
Though the world could give you,
in an instant, the most enticing thing
of all that it offers, and let you see, at
a glance, all the kingdoms of the
earth, and all their glory, could you
possess them beyond the short time
of your life? - Bartoli, Book 2.

March 9.
In our ministry to men, we must
imitate the angels; they do not neglect any means to procure their sal
vation, but the result, whether good
or bad, causes them to lose nothing of
their blessed and eternal peace.
- Ribadeneira, Book 5, ch. 2.

March 10.
You must avoid every vice, but

above all those which tempt you most:
it is in these you will find your great
est danger, if you do not take wise
precautions. - Ribadeneira, ch. 37.

March 11.

If one fears men much he will never
do anything great for God: all that
one does for God arouses persecution.
- Bartoli.

March 12.

Just as we drive out one nail by
another, let us oppose effort to effort,
habit to habit. - Maffaei, *Life of Ignatius
of Loyola*.

March 13.

All creatures are at the service of
God's friends; they help them to acquire greater merit to attach and unite
themselves by a closer affection to

their Creator. - *Letter* 34.

March 14.
With Divine consolation all troubles
change into pleasures, all weariness
into rest. For whoever advances
with this interior peace, is never so
burdened but that it feels light.
- *Letter* 8.

March 15.
He who has renounced the world or
despises it should resemble a statue
which does not prevent itself being
dressed in rags, nor being despoiled of
the purple which ornaments it. - Lancidus

March 16.
It is not enough to say you desire to
serve our Lord: you must declare and
acknowledge fearlessly that you are
His servant and His slave, and that
you would die rather than abandon

His service. - *Letter* 8.

March 17.
The infernal enemy never has more
power against you than when he acts
secretly. - *Spiritual Exercises*.

March 18.
When the enemy cannot succeed in
making you sin, and has lost the hope
of attaining this end, he strives at
least to torment you. - *Letter* 4.

March 19.
One ought not to abstain from the
Bread of Angels, because he does not
feel his sentiments loving enough;
that would be to wish to die of hunger
because one has not honey.
- *Life*, Book 4.

March 20.

It is no less a miracle to see a religious sad, seeking God alone, than to
see true joy in him who seeks all outside of God. - Trinkel, *On the Spiritual
Exercises.*

March 21.

They who live under the rule of
obedience have necessarily all the
more opportunity to advance in perfection, either because God, who is
the Author of perfection, hears their
prayers, or because, as a wise man
has said: "All that man removes
from his own will he adds to his perfection." - *Letter* 51.

March 22.

A precious crown is reserved in
Heaven for those who perform all
their actions with all the diligence of

which they are capable; for it is
not sufficient to do our part well, it
must be done more than well. - Nolarci.

March 23.

I will carefully consider how, on the
day of judgment, I would wish to
have discharged my office or my
duty; and the way that I would wish
to have done it then, I shall do now.
- *Spiritual Exercises*.

March 24.

It is much better to obtain only an
ounce of happiness in not risking our
salvation, than one hundred pounds in
hazarding it. - Bartoli, Book 4, ch. 35.

March 25.

It is a great source of joy for Satan
to see a soul rushing on heedlessly and
deaf to the warnings which would restrain

it; for as much as its pretensions are
exaggerated, so great will be its fall.
- Nolarci.

March 26.
One should neither do nor write
anything from which hatred or
bitterness may arise. - Maffaei.

March 27.
In order that a correction may be
administered with fruit, authority
must be in the one giving it, and
love in the one receiving it. - Bartoli.

March 28.
The only lawful ambition is to love
God, and the price of this love is to
love Him more. - Bartoli, Book 4.

March 29.
A religious ought to dread more being

afraid of poverty than experiencing it.
- Bartoli.

March 30.

Obedience will open for us, beyond
a doubt, the portals of Heaven, which
were formerly closed against us by the
breaking of a Divine commandment,
and which still are shut to whoever is
guilty of the same crime.
- *Letter* 51.

March 31.

I call those thoughts mean which,
in spite of the vain efforts to prolong
them, can only last for a short space
of time; I call those despicable which
extend not beyond this earth.
- Bartoli, Book 2.

APRIL

April 1.
YOU should bring to your praise worthy exercises a holy fervor, because you will feel, even in this life, its good effects, not only in perfecting your souls, but also in the peace of mind you will possess. - *Letter* 50.

April 2.
There are two guarantees of a wise rule of conduct: thought before action, and self-command afterwards. - Martini.

April 3.
If you possess any temporal good, be not a slave to it, but give glory to the Sovereign Master, from whom you have everything. - *Letter* 11.

April 4.

If the love of God burns in your
heart, you will understand that to
suffer for God is a joy to which all,
earthly pleasures are not to be com
pared. - Bartoli, Vol. 1, p. 107.

April 5.

Why so much fatigue to procure
earthly happiness for a soul whose
origin is heavenly, a transient glory for
a soul capable of loving and enjoying
God Himself forever. - Bartoli, Vol. 1, p. 126.

April 6.

They who aspire to reform the morals
of others lose their time and their pains,
by not preaching by example, in
correcting themselves first. - Bartoli, Book 4.

April 7.

You should always manage, as far

as in you lies, that no one may depart
after your sermon less disposed to
peace with God than he was before
it. - *Instruction to Fathers Laynez and
Salmeron.*

April 8.

If we do not feel within us a perfect
patience, we have more reason to pity
the grossness of our nature for being
neither mortified nor dead to the
things of this world, as we should be,
than to blame those who load us
with insults and ignominy. - *Letter* 4.

April 9.

We should not fear much the insults of this life, which are confined
to words; were they all united they
could not hurt a hair of our head.
- *Letter* 4.

April 10.

When the object of our love is infinite we can always love more and more. - *Letter* of April 15, 1543.

April 11.

The acknowledgment of and gratitude for favors and gifts received is loved and esteemed in Heaven and on earth. - *Letter* 34.

April 12.

The first temptation is riches, the second honors, the third pride, and by these three degrees Satan leads us to all other vices. - *Spiritual Exercises*.

April 13.

In the servants of God it is not tne numbers I seek but the merit; I like better to see them distinguish them selves by their deeds than by their

name or habit.
- *History of the Society*, Book 1.

April 14.
Outside of the Church there is nothing truly good; for whoever will not
be united to this mystic body, will
not receive from the Head, who is
Christ Jesus, the Divine grace which
invigorates the soul and prepares it
for eternal happiness. - *Letter* 152.

April 15.
If charity and sweetness have not
truth for their companion they do not
deserve the names of charity and sweetness, but those of hypocrisy and vanity.
- Bartoli, Book 4.

April 16.
In scientific matters there is a manifest
difference between the studious and

the negligent man; now, this difference is the same regarding progress in virtue and victory over the weakness of our nature. - *Letter* 50.

April 17.
One ought to speak little and hear much. - Bartoli, Book 4.

April 18.
In every occupation obedience will help you to advance with increasing merit in the way of perfection, like those who are navigating: for even when resting they are still sailing onward. - *Letter* 51.

April 19.
He who cannot make up his mind to give up all for Christ ought at least to refer all to Him; and to con- sider the highest honors as infinitely

inferior to that one only thing which
our Lord and Saviour has declared
necessary. - Bartoli.

April 20.
What a great right Jesus Christ has
to our service, for the benefits with
which He has loaded us! and how
dear have these benefits cost Him!

April 21.
According as you form a closer
union and friendship with spiritual
men, you will enjoy more happiness
in the Lord. - Orland, Book 5, n. 110.

April 22.
In the face of the never-ceasing
snares of the enemy, it is necessary to
have each day a fixed hour for review,
to enter into one's self and consider
carefully, in presence of God, all one's

thoughts, words, and actions.

April 23.
Imperfect obedience has eyes for
its misfortunes; perfect obedience is
wisely blind; the first passes judgment on the orders it receives, the
second lays aside all judgment.
- Ribadeneira, ch. 33.

April 24.
I call consolation every increase of
faith, hope, and charity, all interior
joy which summons and animates
man to desire heavenly things, and
to wish for his soul's salvation; in
fine, all that which, brings to it repose
and peace in its Lord and Maker.
- *Spiritual Exercises.*

April 25.
Were you to live a hundred years

the possessor of all the kingdoms of
the earth and all their glory, will not
the last day, the last hour finally
come for you? And if you, the possessor for a day of a portion consid-
erably less, were deprived of God for
an eternity, would you gain by the
exchange? - Bartoli, Book 2.

April 26.
All ought to make the holy will of
God the centre and lever of all their
actions, and His Divine qualities the
only object of their discourse, the only
end of their hopes.
- *Summary of the Constitutions*.

April 27.
In order to combat desolation and
put temptation to flight, one ought to
persevere in prayer a little beyond
the prescribed time. Thus he will

accustom himself not only to resist
the enemy, but to overthrow him.
- *Spiritual Exercises.*

April 28.

They who, by a generous effort, make
up their minds to obey, acquire great
merit; for obedience by its sacrifices
resembles martyrdom. - *Letter* 50.

April 29.

By the love and respect we owe
to Jesus Christ our Lord, I beg of
you to begin without delay to amend
your lives with the greatest care, so
that at the last day, when it will be
necessary to give an exact account of
them, you will be found worthy.
- *Letter* 13.

April 30.

In the spiritual life no storm is

more formidable than calmness itself,
nor an adversary more dangerous than
the absence of adversaries. - Bartoli,
Book 2, ch. 18.

MAY

May 1.
In determining on an
enterprise we should offer
it to God, seeing that success must
come only from Him; nevertheless,
in the choice of means and by constant efforts, work as if the entire
success depended altogether on our
selves. - Bartoli, Vol. 2, p. 955.

May 2.
God takes particular care to detach
those from the fleeting pleasures of
this life whom He loves with a love

of predilection, by the desires with which He inspires them for the heavenly life, and by the griefs and afflictions which He sends them in this life. - *Letter* 432.

May 3.
Nothing created can bring to the soul joy equal to that of the Holy Spirit. - Ribadeneira, Book 5, ch. 10.

May 4.
In your dress permit nothing unclean or slovenly, but at the same time avoid a studied elegance, which is not free from daintiness or affecttation. - Bartoli, Book 4.

May 5.
 If you wish to end your undertakings happily, learn how to give yourself up to them without desiring

any return to yourself.
- Ribadeneira, Book 5, ch. 2.

May 6.
Among those who are united in
our Lord Jesus Christ by the bonds
of charity, and by the desire to procure the honor and glory of God,
the most profitable words are those
which the Holy Spirit engraves on
their hearts by the prayers which they
offer for one another. - *Letter* 64.

May 7.
Do nothing, say nothing before
considering if that which you are
about to say or do is pleasing to
God, profitable to yourself, and
edifying to your neighbor.

May 8.
If we were to place on one side of

a scale all the good things created by God, and on the other side all the prisons with all their terrors, the galleys with all their ignominies, the former would in no way counter balance the latter.
- Ribadeneira, Book 5, ch. 10.

May 9.
Be ready to serve those who are least able to help themselves, for the courtier, to gain the favor of an earth ly prince, will often serve him more faithfully than you serve the King of Heaven. - *Letter* 50.

May 10.
Our enemy employs no surer artifice for banishing true charity from the hearts of God's servants, than to make them rule themselves in spirit- ual matters, not with calmness and

reason, but thoughtlessly and with all the unrestrained violence of their passions. - *Letter* 50.

May 11.
When we compare our condition with that of our brethren in India, I cannot see that ours is a hard lot. - *Letter* 114.

May 12.
In dryness as well as in consolations, dangers are encountered if one is not on his guard; if the latter can inspire pride, the former can beget tepidity.

May 13.
Go and set the whole world on fire with the fire of Divine love.

May 14.

We should not only turn our thoughts to Heaven in prayer, but we should accustom ourselves to behold God in everything. - *Life*, Book 5.

May 15.

Meditation and intercourse with God restrain the violence of our unruly nature, and keep its follies within bounds.

May 16.

When one reads a good work by a dangerous author, first the book pleases, then the author himself from that moment, finding the mind predisposed in his favor, he easily inculcates his deadly principles.
- Ribadeneira, ch. 35.

May 17.

It is the tactics of the devil to at
tack a man from without rather than
within; God, on the contrary, rather
moves and forms him interiorly.
- Bartoli, Book 4.

May 18.

They who at the outset count up too
strictly the difficulties and accidents
of an undertaking, or who yield to
fear too easily, will never accomplish
anything great. - Ribadeneira, ch. 37.

May 19.

If only a child profits by my teachings, my trouble and my time will
seem to me well spent.
- Bartoli, Vol. 2, p. 142.

May 20.

It is by acting contrary to the suggestions of the enemy that we will not be deceived, and that the deceiver will be deceived himself. - *Letter* 8.

May 21.

In treating with men we must speak little and hear much; and speak even these few words as if the whole world were to hear them, though we speak only to one. - Bartoli, Vol. 2. p. 254.

May 22.

In loving God for Himself, and man for God, one does what the law commands him, following the saying of St. Paul: "He that loves his neighbor has fulfilled the law." (Rom. 13. 8.) And, indeed, by this very charity which animates him towards his neighbor, he loves God and man at the same time, with the same love. - *Letter* 16.

May 23.

There is no doubt that God will never be wanting to us, provided that He finds in us that humility which makes us worthy of His gifts, the desire of possessing them, and the promptitude to co-operate industriously with the graces He gives us.
- *Letter* 50.

May 24.

Lord, take and receive all my liberty, my memory, my understanding, and my entire will, all that I have, and all that I may possess. Thou hast given me all, Lord, I return all to Thee; all is Thine. Do with these things according to Thy good pleasure. Give me Thy love and Thy grace, these are sufficient for me.
- *Spiritual Exercises*.

May 25.

Whoever desires to act and live in
peace among men, ought to try, above
all, to be good to every one, and injure
no one. - Orland, n. 24.

May 26.

Alas! how vile the earth appears
to me, when I contemplate Heaven!
- Bartoli, Book 4, ch. 28.

May 27.

God gives to each one of us sufficient grace ever to know His holy
will, and to do it fully.
- End of St. Ignatius' *Letters*.

May 28.

Wicked or misinformed men may
calumniate you; pray to God that it
may never come to pass that any one
may speak any evil of you that is not a

calumny. - Bartoli.

May 29.
Let him who finds himself desolate remember how strong he is by grace, which is sufficient to enable him to overcome all his enemies, and that he should take courage in his Lord and Creator. - *Spiritual Exercises.*

May 30.
Place before your eyes as models for imitation, not the weak and cowardly, but the fervent and courageous. - *Letter* 50.

May 31.
To conquer himself is the grandest victory that man can gain. - *Letter* 51.

JUNE

June 1.

THE despising of one's self in
the midst of honors and riches,
and disdain for all glory, should
be esteemed more highly than corporal mortification. - Bartoli.

June 2.

The shortest way, yes, the only way
to reach sanctity, is to conceive a
horror for all that the world loves and
values. - *Examination [of Conscience]*,
ch. 4.

June 3.

It would be the greatest miracle to
see God deny His help to those who,
for love of Him, have given up every
thing. - Bartoli, Book 4.

June 4.

You must practice, at one and the
same time, interior and exterior mortification; but with this difference,
that you must give yourself up to the
first particularly, always, and without ex-
ception; to the second, on the contrary,
only as far as circumstances and the
particular condition of persons and
occasions will permit. - Bartoli, Book 3.

June 5.

The poison which is found in
books soon infects the whole mind,
if one does not check it from the
first. - Ribadeneira. Book 5, ch. 10.

June 6.

We should ask ourselves at the very
outset of our lives, this: What will
God exact of us on judgment day?

What account must we render? So
that we may have for our rule of con
duct His judgment, and not our fancy.
- *Life*, Book 5.

June 7.
God inclines to shower His graces
upon us, but our perverted will is a
barrier to His generosity. - Bartoli.

June 8.
It seems to me that the Divine and
Sovereign Goodness wishes to give you
in His kingdom a most plentiful and
munificent reward for the service you
render Him; since for the good deeds
for which others receive at least a
little consolation in return, even as
regards man, you have known only
pain and most extraordinary contra-
dictions. - *Letter* 172.

June 9.

When God shall have wholly occu
pied our souls in spite of ourselves,
since no one can rob us of our Divine
Treasure, there is nothing in the daily
occurrence of this life which ought to
grieve or worry us much, for every
affliction, whatsoever may be the cause,
only comes from the loss of an object
that one loves, or from the fear of
losing it. - *Letters*.

June 10.

If we confide in God's providence
and resign ourselves entirely into His
hands, and renounce our individual
pleasure, He is pleased to reward us
with great peace and interior consolation, and all the more so if we seek
ourselves less, and more purely desire
the Divine glory and God's good
pleasure. - *Letter* 139.

June 11.

The cowardly, for not wishing to
fight against themselves, will never
enjoy, or only late, true peace of soul
and the possession of any perfection;
the brave and the earnest possess both
in a short time.

June 12.

We do not always rejoice in consolations; but all is for our good,
whether God gives or denies it.
- *Letter* 8.

June 13.

Be assured that in the study of perfection, as in that of the sciences, any
act animated by holy fervor makes
more progress than a thousand others
produced by sloth; so that what the
careless man acquires with trouble,
after many years, the fervent man read-

ily obtains in a short time. - *Letter* 50.

June 14.
God's way in dealing with those
whom He intends to admit the soon
est after this life into the possession
of His everlasting glory, is to purify
them in this world by the greatest
afflictions and trials. - *Letter* 126.

June 15.
If you wish to advance in the love
of God, speak of it; for pious conver-
sations are to charity what the wind
is to the flame. - *Letter* of April 15, 1543.

June 16.
He who forgets himself in the service of God may be assured that God
will not forget him. - Bartoli, Vol. 2, p. 254

June 17.

All that you say in secret, speak as
if you were addressing a multitude.
- Nolarci.

June 18.

If you look into it, you will see that
in times past, when you fell into many
sins, and were less desirous to serve
our Lord, you were neither tempted
nor troubled as much by this serpent,
who is ever seeking to disturb us.
For then your mode of life pleased
Him, while now He cannot endure
the change in you. - *Letter* 13.

June 19.

Although it is sovereignly praise
worthy and useful to serve God by
pure love, we should not less earnestly
commend the fear of His Divine
Majesty. - *Spiritual Exercises.*

June 20.

Hold any man's salvation at
greater value than all the treasures of
the world. - Ribadeneira, Book 5, ch. 8.

June 21.

It is the part of the father of lies to
speak or devise one or more truths,
only to end by an imposture, that he
may entrap us into sin. - *Letter* 66.

June 22.

If, after we have commenced the
practice of virtue, we begin to fear
and lose heart because of the temptations we experience, no beast on
earth becomes so ferocious as the
enemy of our souls, so deep is the
hatred with which he pursues his
wicked designs. - *Spiritual Exercises.*

June 23.

Once our motives are pure and up
right, and we seek not our interests,
but those of our Lord and Master,
He has a constant care over us, be
cause He is infinitely good. - *Letter* 73

June 24.

To use profitably for our neighbor's
salvation the gifts nature has given
us, they must be actuated from
within and draw their strength there
from. - Bartoli, Book 4.

June 25.

We should not measure our spirit
ual progress by our deeds, our amia-
bility, or our love of solitude, but by
the violence we do ourselves. - Maffosi.

June 26.

The successful seeker of souls must

feign blindness to many things; for
once master of the will, he can lead as
he pleases those who practice virtue
under his guidance. - Bartoli, Book 4.

June 27.
That which would have been easily
remedied at first becomes incurable
by time and habit. - Bartoli.

June 28.
Men of great virtue, though of
meager knowledge, incite men more
effectively to virtuous lives by their
words and example, than the greatest
masters of eloquence. - Bartoli.

June 29.
The whole life of religious Orders
depends upon the preservation
of their first spirit. - Orland, Book 6.

June 30.

Be diffident; how powerful is confidence in God! - Ribadeneira, ch. 36.

JULY

July 1.

DO you wish to be always happy?
Then always be humble and obedient.

July 2.

It is characteristic of God and of
His angels to bring to the soul, when
they occupy it, true happiness and
spiritual joy; and to drive from it
the sadness and trials which the
enemy incites in it. - *Spiritual Exercises.*

July 3.

One difficulty of indiscreet fervor

is, that far from subduing the old
man, it subdues the new; that is to
say, it weakens and renders him
incapable of practicing virtue. - *Letter* 50.

July 4.
He who wishes to reach the highest
point of perfection must begin at the
lowest; the height of perfection is in
proportion to the depth of its roots;
and is higher and higher as its roots
are deeper. - Bartoli.

July 5.
To serve the servants of my Lord
is my honor and my glory. - *Letter* 3.

July 6.
We must not speak an idle word,
that is to say, a word which is
not useful, either to ourselves, our
neighbor, or directed to that end.

July 7.

Prudence is not the virtue of him who
obeys, but of him who commands;
the only way to act prudently
in obeying is to give up prudence
sooner than to cease to be obedient.
- Bartoli.

July 8.

There is not a sacrifice sweeter or more
agreeable to God than obedience.
Obedience is better than sacrifice,
says the Scripture. - *Letter* 51.

July 9.

Among the gifts of grace which the
soul receives in Holy Communion,
there is one that must be counted
among the highest; it is that Holy
Communion does not permit the soul
to remain long in sin, nor to obsti-
nately persevere in it. - *Letter* 34.

July 10.

Do not put faith in constant happiness,
and fear most when all smiles upon you.
- *History of the Society*, Book 14, 9.

July 11.

If any one asks you for something
that you believe would be injurious
to him, refuse, but in such a manner
as not to lose his good-will. - Nolarci.

July 12.

What have I done for Christ?
What am I doing for Christ? What
ought I to do for Christ, my Lord and
Savior? - *Spiritual Exercises*.

July 13.

Nothing should influence me to
one decision more than another, except
the service and glory of the Lord
my God, and the eternal salvation of

my soul. - *Spiritual Exercises.*

July 14.

Let superiors take care not to es-
trange their subordinates by severity;
even a suspicion of it does harm.
- Bartoli, Book 3.

July 15.

Pursue with invincible courage the
end to which you have been called;
God has furnished such help and
means to aid you in attaining it.
- Bartoli, Book 4.

July 16.

A soul who desires to make progress
in the spiritual life should always
act contrary to the enemy.
-*Spiritual Exercises.*

July 17.

Obedience not only makes us enjoy
repose, but it ennobles and raises
man above his state; it causes him
to put off himself and to put on Christ,
the Sovereign Good, who is accustomed
to fill all the more that soul which He
finds least taken up with itself; in short,
those who have reached this state have
 a true right to pronounce these words
of the Apostle: "I live, now not I, but
Christ lives in me." - *Letter* 51.

July 18.

I am persuaded that a servant of
God recovered from illness is cured,
partly in order that he may direct and
arrange all the acts of his life to the
glory of God, our adorable Master.
- *Letter* 4.

July 19.
Alas! How men deceive them-
selves, who, thinking they are spiritual,
seek to guide souls! - Bartoli, Book 4.

July 20.
A quarter of an hour's meditation
does more for a man who has con-
quered himself, than one of several
hours for a man still unsubdued.
- Ribadeneira.

July 21.
If our natural feelings, being hurt,
cause us to utter some words, or
to act in opposition with the principles
we profess, we must chastise them
severely until they have obeyed us.
- Bartoli, Book 3.

July 22.
The more a soul enjoys peace and

solitude, the more apt it is to seek and find its Creator. - *Spiritual Exercises.*

July 23.
Here is the difference between the joys of the world and the Cross of Jesus Christ: after having tasted the first, one is disgusted with them, and on the contrary, the more one partakes of the Cross the greater the thirst for it. - Ribadeneira.

July 24.
A great help to advancement in the spiritual life is to have a friend whom you will permit to inform you of your faults. - *Life.*

July 25.
He who has recourse to God, so that He may enlighten him on whatever he asks of Him, whether for a choice

of a state of life, or for any other
spiritual interest, ought first to lay
aside his own will and preference, then
place himself unreservedly in the
hands of the Divine Majesty, with a
full determination of accomplishing
whatsoever His holy will may make
known to him. - Bartoli, Book 4.

July 26.

The apostolic laborer ought to suit
himself to every character: at first, he
should feign and kindly forbear with
many things; but once he has obtained
the good-will of those with whom he
is dealing, he should attack them
with their own weapons.
- Ribadeneira, ch. 37.

July 27.

If you earnestly desire to mortify
yourself in youth, let it be in breaking

your will, and subjecting your private judgment to the control of obedience, rather than in weakening and wounding your body by excesses.
- *Letter* 50.

July 28.
Oh, my God! Oh! if men but knew Thee, they would never offend Thee!
- *Life.*

July 29.
The true peace of God, penetrating the depth of the soul, brings with it every help and grace necessary to secure its salvation and reach eternal life. - *Letter* 15.

July 30.
One does not conquer his anger by flying the cause, but by fighting it.

Solitude does not do away with im-
patience, but only conceals it.
- Bartoli, Vol. 2, p. 176.

July 31.
We should express ourselves in few
words; the truth in all its simplicity
suffices. We should guard against
enlarging on the consequences; truth
in itself always carries conviction;
too many ornaments only weaken and
over-weight it in its struggle with
error. - Bartoli, Vol. 2, p. 127.

AUGUST

August 1.
If God could not be with us on
our altars to expand more
and more freely, day after day, the
sources of His mercy, Jesus Christ,

His only Son, would not exhort us to undertake what His powerful arm alone can aid us to accomplish, when He tells us: "Be perfect as My heavenly Father is perfect."
- *Letter* 50.

August 2.
They who labor in God's vineyard ought to have as it were only one foot resting on earth, the other con- tinually raised to walk in the way of our Lord.

August 3.
Our Lady, deign to intercede for us sinners with thy Divine Lord and Son, and obtain of Him a blessing for us in our trials and tribulations.
- *Letter* 1.

August 4.
I admire those who live in commun-

ity and have a care over one another in mutual remembrance, who are lost to self, that they may be one in God their Creator. - *Letter* 34.

August 5.
Take care that the worldlings do not pursue with greater care and anxiety the perishable goods of this world, than you do the eternal.
- *Letter on Perfection.*

August 6.
One should know, before entering the religious life, that he will not remain there, nor find peace, unless he crosses the threshold with his feet tied, that is, unless he makes a sacrifice of his will and judgment.
- Bartoli, Book 3.

August 7.
It is not enough to love our own souls,
we must have love for all mankind.
- Bartoli, Book 3.

August 8.
To deserve the name of a true religious,
it is not only necessary to renounce
the world, but still more to renounce
one's self. - Bartoli, Book 3.

August 9.
In correcting any one, should kind-
ness fail, use severity, that it may be
useful, at least to others.
- Ribadeneira, Book 5, ch. 7.

August 10.
A crooked and rough trunk of a
tree, if it could think, would never
believe that it could become a statue,

a master-piece of sculpture: it would not wish to place itself under the chisel of any one who, by his art, sees well what he could make of it. Thus many people, hardly living as Christians, are far from imagining that they could become great Saints, if they allowed the grace of God to act in them and not resist its influence.
- Bartoli, Book 4.

August 11.
It is very dangerous to wish to lead every one to perfection by the same path; it is not known how numerous and varied are the gifts of the Holy Spirit. - Quartemius.

August 12.
I do not know a greater happiness than to die for Jesus Christ, or for the salvation of my neighbor. - Nadasi.

August 13.
If men but knew Thee, O my God!
- *Life*, Book 4, ch. 28.

August 14.
As they who endeavor to drive away
a bad thought deserve a great reward
from Heaven, in the same way they
who resist holy inspirations expose
themselves to the danger of falling into
the greatest sins. - Nolarci.

August 15.
Self-love sometimes obscures the
light of intelligence in such a manner
that it makes us consider as impossi-
bilities what in more lucid moments
appear not only easy, but even necessary. - Bartoli.

August 16.
The devil, who has not power over

the soul, is often the author of fanciful imaginations, and uses the body to mislead the souls of such as are naturally vain and fond of novelties.
- Ribadeneira, ch. 37.

August 17.
We must sail against wind and tide, and hope the more as all appears more desperate. - Bartoli, Vol. 2, p. 213.

August 18.
Any tempest which assails us and which we did not bring on ourselves through any fault of ours, foretells a consolation soon to follow it. - *History of the Society*, Book 2, p. 1.

August 19.
In order that you may know how to command and govern others well, you must first be careful to obey, and excel

in the science of obedience.
- *Letter* 51.

August 20.

Love above everything the glory
of God. May God, infinitely good,
be the aim of your words, your
thoughts, and your actions. - *Letter* 1.

August 21.

In speaking to the sad and sore of
heart present to them a cheerful and
serene countenance; speak with all
sweetness, so as to restore them the
more easily to peace and tranquility,
overcoming in this way one extreme
by another. - *Instruction to Fathers
Broet and Salmeron.*

August 22.

One ought to obey a superior, not
on account of his wisdom, goodness,

or other qualities which God has given him, but only because he is God's representative and acts by His authority, who has said: "He that hears you hearsh Me; he that despises you despises Me."
- *Letter on Obedience.*

August 23.
For the love of our Lord let us make generous efforts in His holy service, since we are indebted to Him for so much; we will tire sooner in receiving His gifts, than will He in bestowing them. - *Letter* 1.

August 24.
Treat sinners as a good mother treats her sick child; she lavishes more caresses on him than when he is well. - Bartoli.

August 25.

In martyrdom only the desire to live is sacrificed, but in obedience every kind of desire is sacrificed at one and the same time. - *Letter* 51.

August 26.

May it please the Mother of God to hear the vow I make for you. On condition that you will have patience and perfect constancy, and that there will be no sin on the part of others, I desire, then, that you may receive a great many more humiliations, so that you may have constant opportunities of acquiring new merits. - *Letter* 4.

August 27.

Be careful and do not lightly condemn the actions of others; we must consider the intention of our neighbor, which is often good and pure,

although the act itself seems blame-
worthy. - Bartoli, Book 4.

August 28.
God instructs us in a twofold manner:
in the first He leads us Himself,
but secretly, and therefore, unknown;
in the second, it is man who leads us
by His permission.
- Bartoli, Book 4, ch. 22.

August 29.
Let us often say to ourselves that
wherever we are, or wherever
we may go, even if it be to India, our
loss is not felt. - *Letter* 114.

August 30.
They who fulfill the orders of their
superiors reluctantly and unwillingly
should be classed among the vilest
slaves. - Maffmi, Book 2, ch. 7.

August 31.
Vanity and vain-glory are vices
born of ignorance and blind self-love.
- *Life*, Book 4, ch. 4.

SEPTEMBER

September 1.
NEVER believe an accuser until
after you have heard the accused
and found him guilty. - Nolarci.

September 2.
It is an art as rare as it is precious,
to transact business with many people,
without ever forgetting one's self
or God. - Quartemius.

September 3.
Virtue and holiness of life are not
only all-powerful, or at least very
powerful with God, but also with

men.

September 4.
They who shine by birth, learning, or other qualities, ought to excel in self-denial, otherwise they render themselves more culpable than men without nobility and learning.
- Bartoli, Book 4.

September 5.
He who beholds Heaven with a pure eye, sees better the darkness of earth; for, although the latter seems to have some brilliancy, it disappears before the splendor of the heavens.
- Bartoli.

September 6.
One ought ardently to desire that charm of language so necessary in treating with men. - *Life.*

September 7.

I desire with ardor and more than ardor, if I may thus express myself, that the true love of God may become perfect in you, and that you may consecrate your strength to the service and glory of God our Master, so that I may be able to love and serve you more and more. - *Letter* 3.

September 8.

Oh, no! your heart is not so narrow that the world can satisfy it entirely; nothing, nothing but God can fill it. - Bartoli, Book 2.

September 9.

If you attach your heart to certain places and occupations, it is ten times more likely obedience places you in some other place that you may not like. To be always cheerful, be always humble and obedient. - Bartoli, Book 4.

September 10.
If, one day, I should offend God in any way, or grow remiss, though ever so little, in that which concerns His holy service and glory, I solemnly implore Him, rather let me die. - *Letter* 3.

September 11.
Obedience which ceases at the fulfilling of orders is bad and defective; it does not deserve the name of virtue if it does not rise higher, and make our will and that of our superior one and the same thing. - *Letter on Obedience.*

September 12.
Do not worry yourself over bad, obscene or carnal thoughts, nor about your afflictions or annoyances, when you experience them in spite of your

self. St. Peter and St. Paul were
not able to avoid these trials in all, or
even in part. - *Letter* 8.

September 13.
Every one should try to have his
heart always occupied and filled with
God, to love Him and think of Him
only, and whether alone or with others
never to be out of His presence.
- Bartoli, Vol. 2, p. 6.

September 14.
Idleness begets a discontented life;
it develops self-love, which is the
cause of all our misery, and renders
us unworthy to receive the favors of
Divine love. - *Letter* 10.

September 15.
The errors of others, the portion
left our poor humanity, should serve

to keep us from adding any of ours to them. - Ribadeneira.

September 16.
I do not wish, on my leaving this world, that there be found on me, from head to foot, a single farthing's worth of my own or of others.
- *Letter* 30.

September 17.
They who load us with insults and ignominies give us the means of acquiring treasures more precious than any that man can gain in this life.
- *Letter* 4.

September 18.
Mary's sorrow was less when she saw her only Son crucified, than it is now at the sight of man offending Him by sin. - Nolarci.

September 19.

We often shut the door against the gifts and graces which God wishes to bestow on us, and show very little anxiety about keeping those He has already conferred. - *Letter* 34.

September 20.

It is better to live uncertain of salvation, and meanwhile devote one's self to the service of God and the salvation of souls, than to die at once, with the certainty of entering into everlasting glory. - Bartoli.

September 21.

Let us hold sacred, for the restoration of the sick, all the good things we possess; we who enjoy good health will learn, for lack of better, to content ourselves with dry bread.

- Bartoli, Book 3.

September 22.
Since we have abused the strength
of body and soul to violate the law of
God, we must use, after having recovered grace by repentance, this same
strength to amend our lives.
- Orland, Book 6, p. 1.

September 23.
- Life would be a torment to me if I
discovered, in the innermost depths of
my soul, anything human or not entire
ly Divine. - *Life*, Book 4, ch. 5.

September 24.
It is more difficult to subdue the
spirit than to mortify the flesh.
- Orland.

September 25.
It is not enough to make profession
of a kind of sublime life, if one does
not fulfill perfectly all that such a state
requires. - *Letter* 50.

September 26.
When the devil suggests discouraging
thoughts, we must seek help in the
remembrance of the blessings,
without number, that we have
received from God. - Bartoli, Book 4.

September 27.
That he may prevent us from doing
a good work, the devil often suggests
a greater one; but he understands
well how to prevent its execution
afterwards, by new obstacles.
- *Discernment of Spirits.*

September 28.

Here is the difference between a pious and a frivolous man: the first abstains from pleasure, and is over-whelmed with spiritual consolations; the other gives himself up to the pleasures of the senses, and suffers in his innermost heart. - Nolarci.

September 29.

Such should be our submission to the Church, that if we knew visibly anything to be white, which she had declared black, we should acknowl-edge it black with her.
- *Spiritual Exercises.*

September 30.

Never be severe in respect to those whose virtue is weak; the defiance we might arouse would produce more

evil than any good results we could
hope for from a severe reprimand.
- Bartoli, Book 3.

OCTOBER

October 1.
INNOCENCE and holiness of
life are, of themselves alone, more
powerful and far more preferable
than all other gifts; but without
prudence and the art of dealing with
the world, they remain incomplete
and incapable of guiding others.
- Ribadeneira, ch. 37.

October 2.
If it seems to you that the exact
point, the true medium of discretion,
is difficult to find, I will tell you that

you have a master to teach you; this master is obedience, whose counsels will guide you in the sure way.
- *Letter* 50.

October 3.
Jesus Christ deprived Himself of His happiness, which was infinite, to make us His companions and partakers of it with Him; thus He took upon Himself our miseries to lift the burden from off our shoulders. - *Letter* 50.

October 4.
There is often more danger in making light of little faults than of great sins.
- Ribadeneira, Book 5, ch. 7.

October 5.
How great will be your crown, if besides the obligation you are under to serve God, you add that of working

for the salvation of others, and the honor and glory of God. - *Letter* 50.

October 6.
Labor to conquer yourself. This victory will assure you a brighter crown in Heaven than those gain whose disposition is more amiable.
- *To Edmond Anger.*

October 7.
Paradise and eternity, are they not destined for you? When you desire to conquer them, who will prevent you? When you possess them, who will deprive you of them? - Bartoli.

October 8.
Love ought to consist of deeds much more than of words.
- *Spiritual Exercises.*

October 9.
Truth always shines with a brilliancy
of its own, while falsehood is clouded
in darkness, to dispel which it is enough
to place it in the presence of truth.
- Bartoli, Book 2.

October 10.
Should temptations assail us while in
darkness or sorrow, let us oppose them,
without stopping at the impressions they
make upon us; let us wait patiently for
our Lord to console us. He will banish
all trouble and dispel all darkness.
- *Letter* 8.

October 11.
God desires but one thing of me, that I
submit my soul to His Divine Majesty.
- *Letter* 9.

October 12.

Not only the heavens, but the sight
of a blade of grass, or of the most
insignificant thing, suffices to inflame
with love of God the heart that
knows Him. - Maffaei, Book 3, ch. 1.

October 13.

One might pardon, perhaps, some
neglect in the service of man, but in
the service of God one ought not to
bear with it at any price.
- Maffaei, Book 2, ch. 3.

October 14.

We should confide in God, even to
believing that if a boat were unavailable
to us, the sea itself would afford us a
safe footing. - Maffaei.

October 15.

To win over the world the prudent

fisher of men should be all things to
all men, even though the result should
not be in keeping with his efforts.
- *Life*, Book 5, ch. 11.

October 16.

If one who loves God could be
damned, though not through his own
fault, he could more easily endure all
the pains of hell than the blasphemies
with which the condemned curse God.
- Bartoli, Book 2.

October 17.

By the greater love that we bear
for men of decided and solid virtue,
we ought to punish all the more
severely the least fault in them.
- *Life*, Book 3, n. 36.

October 18.

To win the good-will of men in

God's interest, we must be all things
to all; for nothing is better calculated
to win hearts than a resemblance of
manners and tastes. - Nolarci.

October 19.
God measures His love for a soul by the
degree of union which exists between it
and Himself, and which makes of it an
apt instrument for His designs.
- Bartoli, Book 1.

October 20.
If everything were already known
and assured to us, where would be room
for our confidence in God? Now we
have only the shadow of these things.
Where would be room for hope, if we
possess them already? - Ribadeneira.

October 21.
We ought to place a barrier on the

complainings of our bodies, which, under pretense of weakness, wish to prevent us from laboring.
- Bartoli, Book 5.

October 22.
Before choosing, let us examine well whether the attachment we feel for an object springs solely from the love of God. - *Spiritual Exercises.*

October 23.
The devil sometimes removes all fear from you, only to make you fall; he exaggerates in order to discourage you, and in everything he only seeks your ruin. - Nolarci.

October 24.
He who practices perfect obedience is dead to himself in order to live for God; he is not tossed here and there

by his passions, but resembles a
calm sea, unruffled by the tempest.
- Ribadeneira, ch. 33.

October 25.
Who could count all those who have
had wealth, power, honor? But their
glory, their riches were only lent to
them, and they wore themselves out
in preserving and increasing that
which they were forced to abandon
one day. - Sartoli, Book 2.

October 26.
There is no need of acting ungenerously,
since God is so generous to us.
- *Letter* 3.

October 27.
Put not off till tomorrow what you
can do today. - Bartoli, Book 4.

October 28.

The things of this life are only really happy, as far as they prepare us for the eternal life which follows. - Bartoli.

October 29.

The wicked man easily suspects the virtue of others; as those who have vertigo believe that everything is turning around them. - Maffosi.

October 30.

As much happiness as I felt on learning that the world had insulted you, I felt just as much pain at the single thought, that in your adversity you had sought aid and assistance against the vexation and sorrow which it caused you. - *Letter* 4.

October 31.
What claims has not our Lord to our
service for the blessings He has
showered upon us, and which have
cost Him so dearly! When He proposed
to sacrifice Himself because of His love
for us, He forgot, it seems, according to
our manner of speaking, that He was God.
- *Letter* 50.

NOVEMBER

November 1.
THERE is not among men, nor
even among the angels, an exercise
more sacred, nor a work more
excellent, than to glorify God in Himself, and in creatures by bringing
them to adore and serve Him as far as
they are capable. - *Letter* 50.

November 2.

The unreasonable and excessive man cannot labor for any length of time in God's service; just like the steed that, running immoderately at first, gives out half way in the course, and cannot reach its destination. - *Letter* 50.

November 3.

You postpone this affair for a month, for a year! Ah! how can you count on living that length of time? - *Life*, Book 4, ch. 30.

November 4.

Love the greatest sinners; love them for the little faith they still have, or if they have none, love them for their past virtues; love God's image which they bear; love the precious Blood by which you know they have been redeemed. - Bartoli.

November 5.
Count as the acknowledged enemies
of your soul, sloth, negligence, and
idleness, which cool and weaken the
desire of advancing in piety and
knowledge. - *Letter* 50.

November 6.
I solemnly entreat you, in the name
of our Lord and Savior, who has not
only taught us obedience by word,
but also by example, to love this virtue
with all your heart. - *Letter on Obedience.*

November 7.
God was pleased to ransom us, to
suffer mockery in order to glorify us, to
choose poverty to enrich us, to die in
the disgrace and agony of one condemned to secure for us everlasting
life in the happiness of Heaven.
- *Letter* 50.

November 8.
In certain circumstances it is better
to be silent than to speak. For truth
indicates itself and needs no defense.
- *History of the Society*, Book 15, n. 44.

November 9.
Obedience will enable you to advance
untiringly, and to gain more readily the
road to Heaven; inasmuch as you will
be journeying, in a manner, under the
guidance of an other, and not by your
own will and judgment. - *Letter* 51.

November 10.
In relieving a religious of the multiplicity
of personal cares, *obedience* not only
prevents him from being irresolute and
wavering, but frees him, at the same
time, of the weighty responsibility of
his own will; it compels him to resign
all care of himself, and abandon himself

entirely to the watchfulness of his superiors; from all of which is begotten peace and lasting contentment. - *Letter* 51.

November 11.
Spiritual dryness should not deject us nor consolation make us proud; in the first case we must remember the favors we have already received; and in the second not forget that it is a favor from God, which we have not merited. - Bartoli.

November 12.
Do not form a friendship with any one, unless you know him thoroughly. - Ribadeneira.

November 13.
Adversity is such, that it is really advantageous to the just man, for it causes him a profitable loss; just as a

shower of precious stones might break
the leaves of the vine, but would replace
them by the most beautiful treasures.
- Bartoli.

November 14.
In revealing the defects of others we
make known our own vices.
Examination [of Conscience].

November 15.
If we were to die now, what would
become of us? What account could
we give of all the favors and all the
graces we have received, and of the
many souls lost on our account?
- *Letters.*

November 16.
Ah! that each day I could die a
thousand cruel deaths for Christ and
for the salvation of one single soul! - *Life.*

November 17.
It is better to accustom ourselves to
seek God in everything we do, than
to spend a long time in prayer.
- *Letter* 95.

November 18.
An irresistible incentive to *obedience*
is the loving example of the Man-God,
Jesus Christ, our Lord; who, while
dwelling under the same roof with His
parents, was subject to them; and in
this Holy Family, the Virgin Mary,
Queen of all, was obedient to Joseph.
- *Letter* 51.

November 19.
For the love of Jesus Christ, forget
the past, like St. Paul, and keep
your thoughts incessantly fixed on the
great distance yet remaining before
you reach the way of perfection. - *Letter* 50.

November 20.
He who does not love God with
his whole heart, is loving something
for itself, and not for God. - *Letter* 3.

November 21.
If all things are given as a conse-
quence to those who seek first the
kingdom of God and His justice;
could He fail to give something to
those who seek only the justice of
His kingdom and the King of kings
Himself? - *Letter* 11.

November 22.
Should God accomplish anything
great through our mediation, it
should still make us count ourselves
as nothing, and not cause us to take
the glory to ourselves, for it does not
belong to the instrument, which is
often of little worth, but is due en-

tirely to the hand which directs it.
- Bartoli, Vol. 2, p. 7.

November 23.
In dealing with our neighbor to
keep him from sinning, we ought to
act with the same prudence as with a
man who is drowning, so that we
may avoid the danger of perishing
with him. - Bartoli, vol. 2, p. 7.

November 24.
Since to those who have the will
nothing is difficult, above all as
regards that which they would do for
the love of Jesus Christ our Lord, I
beseech you, then, not to make plans
only, but above all to will their execution
and carry them out. - *Letter* 3.

November 25.
Nothing is sweeter than to love God,

but with a love rich in suffering.
- *Life*, Book 1, n. 55.

November 26.
Just as I will not save myself by the
good works of the angels, likewise I
will not be condemned for the bad and
wicked thoughts which the bad angels,
the world, and the flesh present to me.
- *Letter* 9.

November 27.
We must speak to God as a friend
speaks to his friend, a servant to his
master; now asking some favor, now
acknowledging our faults, and commu-
nicating to Him all that concerns us,
our thoughts, our fears, our projects,
our desires, and in all things seeking
His counsel. - *Spiritual Exercises.*

November 28.

There are always three sure signs of the
good discipline reigning in a religious
house; viz., cleanliness, strict observance
of the cloister and of the rules of silence.
- Lancisius.

November 29.

The rich ought to reach that degree
of perfection of possessing the riches
of which they are the masters, without allowing them to possess them.
- Nolarci.

November 30.

When you behold complete prosperity
reigning anywhere, you may ask yourself
if the service of God is not neglected there.
- *Life*, Book 5, ch. 11.

DECEMBER

December 1.
DISCRETION is necessary in the spiritual life; it is its part to restrain the exercises in the way of perfection, so as to keep us between the two extremes. - *Letter* 50.

December 2.
Those whose circumstances in the world would have assured them an ample fortune, labor in religion with the greater success in promoting the glory of God. - Bartoli, Book 1, ch. 1.

December 3.
Do not think that you injure spiritual progress in that which you grant to the needs of nature. - *History of the Society*, Book 1, p. 1.

December 4.

They who are working for the salvation of souls, ought to seek God's friendship, then man's for God, and regulate their zeal for the honor of God by the advancement of their neighbor. - Bartoli.

December 5.

Resolve never to do anything while moved by passion; wait until it passes away and then take counsel only after mature deliberation. - *Of the Elect.*

December 6.

O my God! O God infinitely good! how can You bear with a sinner like me! - Ribadeneira.

December 7.

If you follow neither rule nor measure, you turn the good into evil, virtue into vice. - *Spiritual Exercises.*

December 8.

It is unnecessary to destroy anything which is good in itself because of its abuses; that would be to impede the work which ought to largely increase the glory of God.

December 9.

In leaving God for God, there is a great spiritual gain and nothing to lose. - Bartoli, Book 4.

December 10.

As God is not the only witness of our life, but as moreover the world, the angels, and men behold it, let us be good not only before God, but also before men. - Ribadeneira.

December 11.

We must praise God in His Saints, as the Psalmist tells us. - *Letter* 3.

December 12.
Obedience is a guide which cannot
err, an interpreter of the Divine will,
which cannot deceive.
- *Summary of the Constitutions.*

December 13.
The greatest reward that a servant
of God can receive for that which he
has done for his neighbor is scorn or
contempt, the only reward that the
world gave for the labors of its Divine
Master. - Bartoli, vol. 2, p. 7.

December 14.
Truth always ends by victory; it is
not unassailable, but invincible.
- Nolarci.

December 15.
If the enemy exalts us, we must
humble ourselves, recalling our sins

and our miseries; if he humbles and degrades us, we must raise ourselves by a true faith and hope in our Lord, remembering the blessings received from Him and considering how, with infinite love and burning heart, He waits to save us. - *Letter* 8.

December 16.
If God gives you much suffering, it is a sign that He wishes to make you a great Saint. - Bartoli, Book 4.

December 17.
May the holy name of our Lord be ever blessed; may it be eternally praised by every creature, who has been created and placed in this world only for that end, so just in itself and so lawfully imposed. - *Letter* 33.

December 18.
The value of a thing is only its
worth before God.
- Bartoli, Book 4, ch. 55.

December 19.
One cannot be the friend of Jesus
Christ, without loving the souls He
has redeemed with His precious
Blood. - Nolarci.

December 20.
They who wish to do great things
in the service of their Lord and King,
will not rest with mere deeds; but
will also wage war against their sensu-
ality, their carnal and worldly love,
and will thus make offerings to Him of
the highest value. - *Spiritual Exercises.*

December 21.
A bow breaks if it is bent too much,

but the soul is lost if it relaxes itself.
- *Letter* 50.

December 22.

We are not the masters of our bodies;
God is; therefore we cannot all
practice corporal mortification in the
same degree. - Bartoli, Book 4, p. 381.

December 23.

We no sooner begin a work for the
honor and glory of God, than the
world at once becomes uneasy, or the
devil throws obstacles in the way.
- Nolarci.

December 24.

Should there be no lurking evils in
a house where peace and tranquility
reign, it is all that can be desired, it
is everything. - Bartoli, Book 3.

December 25.

See God in your superiors; so shall
you learn to revere their will and follow
their commands. Be well assured that
obedience is the safest guide and most
faithful interpreter of the Divine Will. . .
Above all, do not be your own master,
relying on your own prudence, contrary
to the caution of the wise man.

December 26.

He lives happily who, unceasingly,
as far as he is able, has his mind on
God and God in his heart.
- *Life*, Book 3, n. 1.

December 27.

Let us serve God; He will certainly
take care of us and we shall want for
nothing. - Ribadeneira.

December 28.

You wish to reform the world, reform
yourself, otherwise your efforts
will be vain. - Bartoli, Book 3.

December 29.

It is better to be cut off from life,
than to live for vanity. - Nolarci.

December 30.

Do not wait for old age to mortify
your body and your passions. First,
are you sure of reaching it? Again,
how shall you do penance at that age?
- Nolarci.

December 31.

He who by nature is coarse and violent,
and who by dint of resolution becomes
gentle and amiable, often becomes
capable of great and difficult undertakings
in the service of God; because that very

stubbornness, or that natural obstinacy, used in a good cause, knows neither defeat nor discouragement.
- Bartoli, Book 3.

Made in the USA
Monee, IL
30 April 2025

16686129R00069